The Ecstasy of Capitulation

by Daniel Borzutzky

BlazeVOX [books]

Buffalo, New York

The Ecstasy of Capitulation by Daniel Borzutzky

Copyright © 2007

Published by BlazeVOX [books]

Printed in the United States of America

Book design by Geoffrey Gatza

First Edition

ISBN: 1-934289-24-8 ISBN 13: 978-1-934289-24-2
Library of Congress Control Number: 2006938679

BlazeVOX [books]
14 Tremaine Ave
Kenmore, NY 14217

Editor@blazevox.org

publisher of weird little books

BlazeVOX [books]

blazevox.org

2   4   6   8   0   9   7   5   3   1

ACKNOWLEDGEMENTS

I wish to thank the editors of the following journals for originally accepting these poems for publication:

Alice Blue Review, American Letters & Commentary, Aught, BlazeVox, Carolina Quarterly, Chicago Review, Coconut, Dusie, Fence, Golden Handcuffs Review, H_NGM_N, Kulture Vulture, La Petite Zine, LIT, Magazine Cypress, Make Magazine, McSweeneys, Milk Magazine, MiPoesias, Mississippi Review, Near South, Octopus Magazine, Pom², Sentence: A Journal of Prose Poetics, Shampoo, Spoon River Poetry Review, the tiny, TriQuarterly, Typo, and Word For/Word.

Some of these poems also appeared in the chapbook *Rebel Road 5: Poems in the Garden* (w/Brenda Coultas and Marta Lopez-Luaces).

A special thanks to Mark Booth for his friendship, brilliance, and hybrid beasts, and to Jeffrey Kahrs and Amina Cain for navigating. And to my mother and father, for everything.

Table of Contents

TO SUZY

THE ECSTASY OF CAPITULATION

Sharp Teeth of Death: An Essay on Poets and their Poetics

Some years ago, a prospector in a Western state discovered a mine shaft which had been abandoned and sealed off. Thinking there might still be valuable deposits in the mine, the prospector dug his way into the entrance of the old tunnel. After exhausting work, he managed to make a small hole, and crawled into the pitch blackness of the shaft. He found himself in a torturous underground passage in which no man had set foot for years.

The mine was not empty. While the men who dug it originally had abandoned the shaft, the poets had not. When the mine was sealed, hundreds of poets, imprisoned and captured for participating in the worst forms of social deviance, were sealed into it. They had nothing to eat in the black tunnel except each other. When the lone man crawled in among them, the poets were starving. They attacked him savagely.

There was no one to hear the man's agonized screams, no one to help him fight off the hordes of ferocious poets. When the poets had finished their grisly work, little was left of this unfortunate prospector.

This story is told to illustrate the ferocious savagery of poets. Almost unnoticed, poets have continuously battled the human race for domination of the earth. This unrelenting foe has fought a vicious war against humankind for hundreds of years, and they still might win it.

The case of the prospector is by no means the only example of poets attacking human beings. Here in the United States, thousands of babies have been bitten and even killed by poets who invaded their cribs with verse only to maul the babies with their teeth after they responded with tears and cries of agony. In Western countries, where people live in relative luxury, the toll taken on human flesh by poets and their poetry is fantastic.

But direct attack is not the only way poets carry on their relentless war. The numbers of human beings they kill with their teeth are as nothing compared to the hundreds of thousands they have killed by scourging the world with the insidious abomination of their verse. The Romantic Poets, the Modernists, the Confessional Poets, the New York School, the Language Poets, the School of Quietude, the Post-Avant, Flarf, time and again, poets carrying plagues have scurried off ships in new ports, and within days have started a holocaust of excremental writing. Readers have vomited in the streets; men and women have run screaming from their homes; parents have abandoned their children; and youngsters have fled from their parents at the sight and sound of the words spewed by poets.

But hysteria and nausea are only two of the conditions transported by poets to humans. General adaptation syndrome is another, as well as bed-wetting, fetishism, exhibitionism, histrionic personality disorder, intermittent explosive disorder, insomnia, narcissistic personality disorder, panic attacks, premature ejaculation, sadism, delusional disorder, agoraphobia, flatulence, and amnesia.

Poets have also been known to viciously murder chickens, geese, cows, elk, deer, dogs, cats, and buffalos merely to write sestinas and villanelles with the blood they collect from the dead carcasses. In this way, poets not only inflict social but economic losses on their human enemy by robbing them of food they may need for survival.

There is no question that civilization's worst enemy is the poet, who outdoes all wild beasts in destruction of lives and property. Poets cause more damage than all other tyrants combined.

Yet despite all the resources of modern science and American know-how, we are losing the fight to destroy this enemy.

One reason for this steady retreat in the war against poets is the enormous fecundity of these savage animals. Poets breed poems more rapidly than they can be destroyed. About three and a half million poems are born daily in the United States, and within a year one poet will average fifty to sixty offspring. In most cities, there are at least as many poems as there are people.

It is impossible, of course, to take a "poet census" for no one really knows how many of these savage enemies are crawling unseen all around us. Bloom and Vendler relate the efforts of early scholars to estimate the poet population. For example, about a hundred years ago, in Paris, special traps were set in horsemeat factories. The owners complained that poets were destroying every scrap of meat. Two thousand six hundred poets were captured in one night and, within a month, the total came to sixteen thousand.

One year in New York City, when the invasion was at its worst, authorities offered the traumatized populous a reward for killing the poets. The aroused population went on a crusade, and within a short time twelve thousand poets were captured and executed.

In Frankfurt, during one plague, city officials paid one *pfenning* for every dead poet brought to them. They cut off the left hands of the poets as a way of keeping their accounting straight, and threw the corpses into the river.

Scientists in modern times have designed effective poisons as well as other techniques for killing poets, but authorities admit that these antidotes alone cannot do the job. None of the techniques so far available are effective enough to conclusively wipe out these most vile and repugnant of vermin.

Poets are hardy, fearless, ferociously savage, insatiably hungry, and thoroughly destructive; they climb, swim, and gnaw their way through civilization so it is all but impossible to keep them out of any place they wish to enter.

Unlike many other pests, nothing favorable can be said about poets. Even the thought of eating them is horrifying to humans, although we eat almost all of our other enemies, such as lions, snakes, and even other men and women. If we could only bring ourselves to eat poets, the poet problem would be solved simply by turning them into a table delicacy. The human race has eradicated a great number of its animal neighbors, both friendly and unfriendly, through the simple expedient of converting these beasts to food.

It is not likely that poet meat will ever become so popular that the desire for profit will cause them to be hunted, as men have hunted wild turkey and pheasants almost to their extinction. However, it must be said, that poets *can* be eaten. During the siege of Paris, almost one hundred years ago, the bodies of poets brought a high price when offered for sale to the starving population.

The war on poets goes on. How many of these vicious secret agents are aligned against us we cannot know. How we are going to defeat this enemy is also unknown. In the meantime, poets have an almost free hand—invading, devouring, destroying, and killing.

Where will it end? It may well end in the destruction of civilization, if not by the poets themselves, then by the poets in combination with other destructive forces which humans choose to nourish in the bosom of culture. And in that fatal combination, the fierce and insatiable poet will not be one of the least factors in the final end of human life on our planet.

Sexual Pressure

Alan, a participant in the men's "Fear of Failure" workshop,
says, When we are making love, I often see my wife in a hair
shirt. Dwarfs, twenty-seven inches high, dwell in the mind of Thomas,
who has practiced masturbation since an early age but never felt

Comfortable with women. About a month ago, says Mona,
my boyfriend and I acted out a rape fantasy of mine. Even
though we had it all mapped out, I freaked. I yelled at him to stop but
he thought it was part of the game and kept going. Afterwards he

Felt terrible, and now I don't want to have sex with him. Of course,
a moment's reflection shows more than meets the eye. For perhaps it
is our own feverishness preventing us from being properly
satisfied. Everything that understands itself is distorted, and in

The complementary world of our imagination we may
often see our lovers as goats with human heads, as human
bodies with fish heads, as winged monsters with hooked beaks, as vultures
and crabs and griffons. I once dated a man, says Tina, who occasionally

Lapsed into a weapon-bearing maiden. He made me squeal with pleasure
but when we finished making love he wouldn't speak. Men aren't always
comfortable talking about feelings, says Lesley Di Mare, Ph. D.
And since everything a man has to say is implied in his behavior,

With the help of a word here and there, don't sweat the small stuff.
Sometimes, says Elizabeth, when my husband can't get it up I feel as
if I'm a river whose waters are being kidnapped by merchants
or marauders. At first my husband was a marauder, but now

He is an arthropod who settles on the water and dies. Gently,
I lift his corpse into the air, and sing softly as he floats
towards heaven. This is not an uncommon phenomenon,
explains Laura Corn, author of *52 Invitations to Grrreat Sex*.

When this happens, lean in close to his ear and softly command him
to kiss you harder or bite your neck. This will redirect his erotic
attention because it appeals to his instinct to please you.

Sexual Knowledge

Clare never doubted that her husband Phil loved her. But for most of this
couple's married life he hadn't been interested in having sex more than
twice a month. When pressed for details, Phil admitted
he had been an excessive masturbator and this perhaps was the reason for his
lack of desire. So, thought Clare, masturbation—that's the way out. And

She proceeded as many women do to use the urethra for this purpose. Numerous
tricks were tried, none of which satisfied her, though they rekindled the interest
of her husband. Maybe it's the internal porn reel we continually play in our heads,
said Phil, but a woman who isn't shy about laying a hand on herself is just hot.

One of the biggest complaints couples have is that they are existing in a state of living
death; it is a perpetual torture and some relief must be afforded or the end will be
an insane asylum from self-abuse. In many cases relief can only be obtained by
continued and severe whipping. This form of sexual perversion can often be traced
to the painful experiences of early

Childhood. But in the words of Louis Redmond[1], Little Girls who have become
tarnished can be restored by immersion in a solution of soap and water. They
appear to enjoy this treatment and will come out looking brand new. They differ in
this respect from little boys, who are not fully washable and who shrink in self-esteem
if placed in water. Every Little Girl should be taught to understand a boy's need for a

Protective coating of grime. Otherwise she may in later life commit such errors as
burning her husband's bathrobe as it is about to become broken in. Neither the
mills of the Gods nor the mortar and pestle of the apothecary can grind out a prescription
to assist in the act of love. The good news is, says Carol Rinkleib Ellison, Ph.D.,
sex can get better. If you want more and better sex the key may be, paradoxically,

To lower your expectations, touch your husband every day, hold hands, snuggle during
the evening news, put the dog in the other room, unplug the phone, lock the bedroom
                                                                     door,
slip your tongue in his mouth and cup his butt. Men don't have a lot of testosterone to
                                                                     begin with,
and people have so few hours at home together that sometimes sex seems like just another
                                                                     job
to perform. The sexual life can be Heaven or Hell—let us strive for the former.

---

[1] Louis Redmond, "What I Know About Girls," *Coronet*, 1952

Are Nudists Nuts?

after Elton R. Shaw, "Are Nudists Nuts," *Sex: Sane Sex Standards*, June 1935

King Saul was a nut. He stripped off his clothes and
prophesied before Samuel. Jesus was probably a nut.
Disciples were nuts. When they were fishing they were often nude.
They saw nothing improper in disrobing because in some occupations
nudity was common.

Isaiah was a nut. The Lord told Isaiah to be a nudist and he was one for
three years. The Lord told Isaiah to loose the sackcloth off his loins and the
shoes off his feet and Isaiah did so, going naked and barefoot. Thus by the
prophet walking naked and barefoot three years was the shameful captivity of
Egypt and Ethiopia prefigured.

Early Christians were nuts. Historians of the early church tell us that
in the outdoor ceremonies the rite of baptism was administered to
candidates in the nude. Also, the nude bodies of early Christians were oiled
during purification ceremonies. Many outstanding ministers of our day
are nuts. The outstanding pioneer in German nudism was a Lutheran Minister.
The nudists are not nuts. The nuts are the people who are slaves to the

Superstitions of the obscenity of the human body.
According to one nut, members of a tribe accustomed to nudity, when made
to assume clothing for the first time, exhibit as much confusion as would a
European compelled to strip in public. Another nut adds that nothing would
make for avoidance of potbellies and other acquired deformities as nudity would.

What good are clothes? Clothing tends to make men bad. Judge B.
Linsey wishes the day might come when we might strip every stitch
from our bodies anywhere at anytime without shame.

The human body in action, as in a graceful dance, or in athletic exercise,
brings elements of esthetic enjoyment to the spectator.
Nudists are nuts. Let's take them to Africa and let them run around with baboons
and monkeys. What is a nut? When you've bats in your belfry, if your
comprenezvous rope is cut. If you've nobody home in the top of your dome
then your head is not a head; it's a nut.

Noun Clause

The understanding of what I do not understand
is the understanding that I cannot understand
what I understand when I understand
what I cannot understand. When I understand
what I cannot understand, I understand that not only
must I understand that I am trying to not understand
but I must also understand that to not understand
is to understand, and that to understand is to not understand.
How can I understand
that to understand I must not understand? How can I understand
that I must both understand
and not understand at the same time? Concerning this,
a man once said, Imagine that you understand, and
that this understanding is more powerful than anything
you could ever understand. If you possess this understanding
it will disappear into you, become part of you, and
you will no longer understand. But if
you do not possess this understanding, you will possess
this understanding, it will disappear into you,
become part of you, and you will no longer understand that
you do not understand and, at the same time, you will
understand that you no longer understand, and only then
will you understand that to understand is to not understand
what you understand when you say that you do not understand.

Present Progressive

The conversation we are having, she said,
is about the conversation we are having,
though it is not the conversation I want
to be having about the conversation we
are having. I do not know, exactly, what
conversation I want to be having about
the conversation we are having, she said,
I only know that we are not having it; though,
to be truthful, she said, I do not want
to be having the conversation I want to be
having about the conversation we are having,
which is to say, she said, that I am afraid of
the conversation I want to be having. Conversely,
she said, I am not afraid of the conversation
we are having, by which I do not mean to imply
that the conversation we are having
brings me comfort. The conversation we are having
about the conversation we are having brings me
no comfort, she said, which is to say that it
is more comfortable to be afraid of the
conversation we are not having than it is
to not be afraid of the conversation we are
having, which is to say, she said, that when I say
I am not afraid of the conversation we are
having about the conversation we are having,
I am actually more afraid of the conversation we are
not having about the conversation we are having,
and when I say that I am afraid of the conversation
we are not having about the conversation we are having,
she said, what I mean is that I am less afraid of the
conversation we are having about the conversation we are having.

Simple Present

I only think of you when I do not
think of you. Conversely, when I
think of you, I do not think of you.
Of course, when I think of you, I
think of you, but the you I think of when I
think of you is not the you I want to think of.
The you I want to think of is the
you I think of when I do not think of you.

Ronald Reagan in Berlin

Dear Mr. Gorbachev, if we are together
Again do not spank me upon my bare buttocks.

For spanking my bare buttocks causes blood to
Collect there and in the adjacent genital

Regions. This abnormal flow of blood to the
Area stimulates my tissues and nerves and

Creates a distinct reaction. Now, Mr.
Gorbachev, when my sex impulse becomes

Stimulated I associate the sensation
With that of spanking and whipping and often

I find it necessary to experience
A beating before the sex reaction can be

Produced. Last night, Mr. Gorbachev, I dreamt I
Was a stallion who produced both male and female

Sex hormones. Nancy was a castrated male dog
Who attempted to nurse young puppies. And you,

Mr. Gorbachev, were a caponed hen who ceased
To crow, grew a cocks-comb and attempted

Husbandry with other hens. Afterwards, Mr.
Gorbachev, we spoke intelligently to ducks,

Geese, puppies, rabbits, kittens, and chipmunks.
We also got along with taciturn types such

As snails, worms, beetles, and toads. Liberalization,
Mr. Gorbachev, is how we were able to understand

The language of these little animals. Tear down this
Wall, Mr. Gorbachev. Thank you, and God bless you all.

Richard Milhous Nixon's First Inaugural Address

for Mark Booth

Senator Dirksen, Mr. Chief Justice, Mr. Vice President, President Johnson, Vice President Humphrey, my fellow Americans—and my fellow citizens of the world community.

I ask you to share with me today the majesty of squirrel-headed otters. In the orderly transfer of species, we celebrate the unity that keeps us free. Each moment in history is war, fleeting and unique. But some stand out as wars of beginning, in which hybrid beasts are shaped by the convergence of unmatched body parts. This can be such a moment.

Penguin-headed dogs are walking in space and for the first time we see that man's deepest aspirations will at last be realized. The spiraling evolution of humanity allows us the possibility of combining animals, of unions between gorillas and hippos, advances that once would have taken centuries. In throwing wide the horizons of failure, we have invented new breeds on earth. For the first time, because the people of the world want combinations of animals, and the leaders of the world are afraid of humans, the times are on the side of peace. What kind of beasts shall we combine—what kind of combinations shall we choose, whether we combine with new techniques or old—is ours to determine by our actions and our choices.

The greatest honor history can bestow is the abolition of honor. This honor now beckons America—the chance to invent animals who will help the world out of the valley of turmoil, and onto that high ground of centaurs and chimeras that men have dreamed of since the dawn of civilization. If we succeed, generations to come will know that we mastered our moment, that we helped make the world safe for hybrids and humans alike. This is our summons to greatness.

The second third of this century has seen the flourishing of kakapos and karakuls. We have seen brave chimpanzees defend their holy cities with ingenuity. We can be proud that we are better educated, more afraid, more passionately driven to create chickens whose feet are the hands of apes; ostriches whose legs are the legs of antelopes; armadillos whose ears are the bronchial tubes of giraffes.

John Adams said that though we have lost sight of our enemy, we have found ourselves in the midst of an *epouvantable orage*.[1] In our time, we have found ourselves not in the midst of an *epouvantable orage* but in the midst of an epizootiological conundrum. 375,000 British horses were killed during the First World War. This resulted in the loss of 1,500,000 legs. If these legs had been found, they could have been attached to the bodies of adolescents and infants, to sea-lions and sheep. We see in Mr. Ed, the talking horse, who made his first appearance only 8 years ago, how close we have come to what we seek

---

[1] Thunderous storm

to achieve. Riders on the earth together, let us go forward, firm in our faith, steadfast in our purpose, cautious of the dangers, but sustained by our confidence in the will of God and the promise of man.

Henry Kissinger's Acceptance Speech for the 1973 Nobel Peace Prize

Though I deeply cherish the dickcissel and the ionization chamber
Given to me by the members of the committee, I thank them most for
Allowing me this opportunity to speak the language of peace, which
Has nothing in common with human language, except for certain words
Resounding from particular affections. But in this age of
Thermonuclear technology, the language of peace must be brought into
The mouths of humans, whose rigid tongues are not used to the gentle tones of
Angels. *Usi teluto pingofo mapate, sasafu fasu*
Imfose, said the angel Fuloto to me in my sleep last night. I
Cannot translate literally. The best I can do is to say that
Fuloto asked that you each ride the chariots of your
Minds into the perfect vacuum of intuition, where a buttered
Fish awaits you.

There are several people I must acknowledge and without whom I would
Not have received this award. To the international community
Of mimes and court jesters, who bring needed levity to politicians as we
Wander over hostile lands ever-shaken by tremors, inhabited
By awesome beasts, I salute you, and accept this gift in your honor. And
To my personal troop of interpretive dancers—who have
Accompanied me on diplomatic missions with nincompoops, I give you my
Sibilant, semi-vocal prayers. They will arrive while you are dreaming and,
Like the birds of Aristophanes, they will make you say:
Hoop-ahoy! Hoop-hip a-hoop-hip ahoy!

But as the hour is running late, and as one can never acknowledge all
Who have improved the world, let us turn our attention to
Eskimos. Delicate and ever-fleeting, they are non-gray creatures we
Must embrace like Johnny-Come-Lately's of the Arctic.
When faced with social and political discontent, they developed an
Understanding of fashion sense quite unique and admirable. Last year,
In an igloo, a representative of their people gave me a large
Orange tray with a vanilla hued-top. *(holds up tray)* This lacquered unit
Has a Creamsicle effect and is perfect for cocktail wieners, skewers of
Lemon-grilled chicken, and even martinis. At a recent meeting with my
Chinese counterparts, we struggled to understand the goals of each other's
Nations, but we shared a common pleasure, eating pastry puffs and egg rolls
Off these glorious serving dishes. By now you
Have surely seen the photographs of Chairman Mao Tse-tung holding one end of
The tray while I grasped the other. Our hands walked across this bridge

Between nations and met in a firm shake of unity.
I have informed President Nixon of these fantastic trays and
He has assured me that he will order hundreds of them for the White House.
Moreover, he has made these trays a fundamental part of his structure
Of peace, a peace to which all nations have a stake and therefore to which all
Nations have a commitment.

We are seeking a sophisticated, tasteful world, not as an end to
Itself, but as a vehicle for the realization of man's
Noble aspirations of tranquility and community. If style,
Then, is to be our common destiny, then style must be our common
Practice. For this to be so, the ladies of all nations must
Wear glossy boots, enamel-coated bangles, and
Strikingly minimalist skirts, shawls, and handbags. They must remember that
Their fashion decisions are realized in the well-dressed nature of their
People. They must remember that peace flows directly from thoughts of peace,
As if the thoughts simply projected themselves. And thoughts of
Peace, my friends, flow much more smoothly when men of broad vision accessorize
Their suits with silk handkerchiefs manufactured in
Civilized nations, whose citizens must not be merely concerned with the
Fashion sense of individuals, for if lasting peace is to come, it
Will be the accomplishment—not of a well-dressed man or a well-dressed
Family, or even a well-dressed nation—it will be the accomplishment
Of a well-dressed mankind. With these thoughts, I extend to you
My most sincere appreciation for this award.

Education Policy Speech

We must support those around the world taking risks to eradicate contracted furrows through legislative measures designed to punish owners of flaking faces who refuse to wage war on the inevitable effects of nature. Our policy must be clear and consistent in its purpose. We must stand by those young women who scream in disbelief upon hearing that once there was a time when wrinkles kept with dignity their crinkled place beneath the eye.

The courage of those multitudes of ordinary citizens who describe their favorite aspect of boredom as that time in the afternoon when millions of people are hopeful that the moon will prevail as it does each night signals the arrival of an entirely different era. We must do everything in our power to foster these views, and to embrace those former experimental poets turned bureaucrats who cut out their own tongues in search of the promised land where words are meant to mean what they mean. Remembering what we saw that morning when those tongues were chopped up and stirred into our cereal, we have as clear a responsibility as could ever fall to a democracy: We must do everything in our power to protect our people from those individuals in focus groups who confess that when they picture themselves as fire-breathing dragons, they blow fire out of both their mouths and buttocks. *(applause)*

This great and urgent responsibility has required a shift in national policy. For the majority of the past century, we have treated the sadism of academicians as isolated cases. Even after an assault inside our own borders—when throngs of nomadic community college professors were filmed flogging pelvis-thrusting administrators on blood-stained sheets atop vibrating mattresses in suburban Red Roof Inns—there was a tendency to treat these sordid scholars as individual criminals, to be handled through law enforcement. These scholars were tracked down, arrested, convicted, and sent off to serve 140-year sentences. Yet behind this act was a growing network of operatives, devoting their days to the service of pedagogy by pulling corpses out of tombs, stabbing those corpses repeatedly until finally the corpses awoke from the dead and sang: We died so that we could be dead, but now that you have killed us we are alive, alive, alive.

Against this kind of determined, organized, ruthless enemy, we require a new strategy with several key elements. These rogue scholars have no boundaries, defend no ideologies, and are unconstrained by accepted rules of conduct. Such an enemy cannot be reprogrammed to meet our criteria. Such an enemy can only be eaten, ladies and gentlemen, and this is the business at hand. *(applause)*

As we speak, ladies and gentlemen, we are marinating in secret cells those tenured members of the Economics, Sociology, and English Departments. Of those known to speak multiple languages, most are now covered in olive oil, lemon juice, and garlic, and they will be filleted and skewered before the others. The social sciences and humanities have sustained heavy losses, and they will sustain more.

And we are applying a special sauce. It is one of those condiments that most take for granted but have no clue about its origins. We stored it for many years, and have only recently rediscovered it during a clean-up mission after a graduation ceremony at one of our so-called institutions of higher learning. Sealed in air-tight wooden casks, the ingredients had mixed into a wonderfully flavored concoction which was bottled and quickly became a hot item with the rank and file members of our intellectual-eating brigade.

The first to be soaked in this special sauce were the members of the Honor Society. Disinclined to participate in athletics, they were not as meaty as some might have liked, but I personally found them quite flavorful, complemented as they were by a full-bodied South American wine.

After that first banquet, we took another essential step in the war on education. This time, in the weeks before grilling, we injected our scholars with a balsamic vinaigrette serum which made them less likely to use words to describe thoughts or feelings. And those who did speak, we stuffed their mouths with cilantro-infused lamb burgers. We thought: if those we eat are well-fed, then we too shall be well-fed. We were correct in this judgment, and when we brushed these free thinkers with sauce, and locked them in our preservation chambers, we sang with glee as moral decrepitude dripped like gravy off their bodies. So proud we were to lick them.

All citizens, regardless of political affiliation, can be satisfied with how we have dealt with our academicians. And I have been humbled to work with a staff who has shown, in its conduct, the optimism, strength, and decency to capture the residents of our universities, and to serve them in new and innovative ways.

Thank you for your continued support. *(applause)*

Congressman Proposes English Language Unity Act

We strive in contest against difficulties through a single common combination of characters period thus we create enduring and cooperating social groups whose members have developed organized patterns of relationships through oral interactions period in this regard comma we stand in definite contrast to other territories piercingly separated into parts or pieces by dissimilar combinations of characters period

Here in our definite territory we have the state or quality of being in accord due to the fact that we use one common combination of characters period but there are aggregations of single units in our definite territory who do not use our common combination of characters comma thus invalidating their ability to contribute to our network of structures in which single units have the capacity to perform or act effectively and authoritatively period

Allow the speaker to share a narrative related to him by a single unit pertaining to an act in violation of the body of rules and principles governing the speaker's particular district period the single unit was from a landlocked country of Western Africa comma a former French protectorate whose capital is Ouagadougou comma or perhaps now no the single unit was a native of a Slavic republic settled in the 6th or 7th century comma Christianized in the 9th century comma independent in the 13th century comma dominated by foreign powers in the 14th century comma independent in the late 19th century comma dominated again by foreign powers in the early 20th century comma and independent in the late 20th century period the single unit produced the following combination of characters colon

The otter dairy I went to cornea cafetorium to buy skimpy handmade latte but cleric did not speak anguish he only spoke vulgarian and I could not find skimpy handmade latte I only found holy capuchin and because I don't speak vulgarian I could not say to cleric that to brought in more customers is necessary to half skimpy handmade latte moral of story is gang men two months later rubbed cleric who also cash ear and did not stand under gang men who speak Latin and need creamy fill-ins for sweet stick period

In other words comma the speaker attempted to purchase an ungenerously proportioned lactose beverage prepared by the terminal part of the human arm located below the forearm but the member of the clergy did not utter agonizing physical or mental pain comma he only uttered sound combinations marked by a lack of good breeding comma the result being that the speaker did not have the ability to ascertain through observation the aforementioned ungenerously proportioned lactose beverage comma he only ascertained through observation a religious hooded cloak worn by the sex that produces ova and bears young period due to the absence of a common combination of characters comma the speaker could not communicate to the member of the clergy that in order to have a greater number of individuals purchasing goods or services comma it is imperative that the premises possess the aforementioned ungenerously proportioned lactose beverage period the principle contained in the fable is that on a subsequent date a groups of hoodlums banded together to apply pressure and friction to the member of the clergy comma which was incapable of rising to an upright position period

Single units and aggregations of single units who plead in favor of using two or more combinations of characters in order to facilitate the acquisition of information and experience by young units who pursue knowledge believe that inhabitants of our definite territory ought to have fees or dues levied upon them to establish or organize distinctly bounded areas that employ combinations of characters that do not belong by nature period

The speaker has distinguished the flavor of the whitish liquid containing proteins comma fats and various vitamins and minerals produced by the domesticated bovine with two fleshy muscular organs attached to the floor of its mouth period it has a tart and tangy taste comma like that produced by acids period

The Ecstasy of Capitulation

I.

One reason to eat is to not speak, said the man
with a mouth full of food. When she told me that my

silence was worse than her silence, I agreed,
even though she was wrong. It is shallow to fight

for things, he said, but sometimes it can be fun. You
look like a tunnel, she said, and kissed my lips. What

I like least about words is their capacity
to invoke more words, she said, as she trashed my

poem. According to the *New York Times*, gay
teenage boys want monogamy while

heterosexual boys prefer "friends with
benefits." My psychiatrist told me it was

okay to lie about the important details
of my life. As a result, I fell in love with

her. I stopped seeing her as a patient but when
we dated the spark was gone. If, as Cioran writes,

existing is plagiarism, then what is death?
I was lost all night in the forest only to

discover these were streets I knew quite well. In the
Oresteia, Apollo argues that the true

parent is "he who mounts." Because the Furies fail
to ask what happens when the woman is on top,

they lose the case. In evaluations, a
student wrote: "Daniel would be a better teacher

if he wasn't such an asshole." Weren't such an
asshole, I wanted to tell her, though as her

comments were supposed to be anonymous, I
could not admit that I recognized her

handwriting. On a first date, I innocently
went to the bathroom when the check arrived. She thought

I was trying to stick her with the bill but when
she realized I was unaware of dating

etiquette she was charmed. We had a nice kiss
goodnight, but afterwards I was so flustered I
went to a bar by myself, drank whiskey, and smoked
my first cigarettes in years.

II.

> *Throughout my life I have always wanted to tell the truth,*
> *even though I knew it was all a lie. In the end all that matters*
> *is the truth content of a lie.*
>
> —Thomas Bernhard, *Gathering Evidence*

Before I met Lisa in person, says Jerry,
a user of an online dating service, I
really enjoyed the wit and flirtatiousness of
her emails. But on our first date she was stiff as
a board. I wasn't attracted to her, though I
slept with her anyway, just in case I might like it.
And I did. I liked it so much, that now we're
getting married.

I love you, she said, as she smacked her child's head.

I love you for your holes, she said,
not just the holes in your shoes and socks, but the
gaping holes in your personality.

When she asked me if I was uncomfortable,
I told her I wasn't.
I really was uncomfortable.
What I neglected to say
was that I enjoy being uncomfortable.

Two old friends meet in a café to discuss
mutual funds and stock options. Thus begins a
story that ends with one man slicing off the
other's neck, and stuffing his mouth with love poems
to Young Werther.

Life is too short to be genuine,
he said, as he stared into her deep
brown eyes. It was the most genuine thing
he'd said all day.

The Performance of Becoming Human

The lateral concept of evening entered the
bilateral talks between day and dawn. Who shall
descend into the sky from the sky above the
sky, he said. Who shall desist from not seeing the
visible by focusing on the
invisible, she said. These days, she said, I think
often of the relationship between
inflection and substance. He told me he loved me,
she said, but he said it the wrong way. I
thought I said I loved her the right way, he said, but
it came out stiff and awkward. I told her I loved
her, he said, and she looked at her watch. Time flips when
you're standing on your head, he said. Time slips when you're
wasting a certain type of time, he said. I like
to waste eternal time, she said, by which she meant
that the most important concepts are the ones we
remember the least. On the surface, she said, we
danced with the history of looking beneath the
surface. A surface reading of looking beneath
the surface, he said, reveals more about what rubs up
between the seen and the unseen. The word friction,
he said, contains the word fiction, and the word
fiction, she said, means the opposite of not not
true. The question of happiness comes up
regularly, he said, but we never know how to
answer it. We should replace the question of
happiness with a mental image of a long
slippery slide, she said. Memory is the
sliding scale by which we decide how much stock to
invest in the present, he said. Alone with a
depressed student in my office, he said, I made
him promise not to kill himself until he turned
30. My mother made me promise not to get
a tattoo until I turned 25, she said.
When I turned 25, she said, I still wanted
a tattoo, but I didn't get one because I
was afraid of offending my mother. The fear
of offending, he said, makes us all too aware
of how easy it is to lose those we love. I
told him I loved him, she said, but I'm not sure what
I meant. She told me she loved me, he said, and then
she ran to the bathroom and stayed there for a long

time. In the bathroom, she said, I thought of a man
I knew who became more human by
volunteering to kill animals at the
shelter. Men often imitate animals, he
said, and then they call this art. I thought of Kafka's
ape, she said, who becomes human by
imitating men who spit and belch. I told him
I loved him, she said, and then I ran to the
bathroom and thought of how animals love each
other. When she came back from the bathroom, he said,
I asked her if she felt okay. He asked me why
I had been in the bathroom for so long, she said,
and I told him I was sorry. When she came back
from the bathroom, he said, she asked if I'd ever
been to the circus. I told her I loved her, he
said, and all she wanted to talk about was
animals. Men swing around like monkeys, she said,
and this makes them feel more human.

590 AM

The talk show host was happy to see that pigeons were finally making a contribution to society, and he wanted to know if we, the listeners, had any problems with pigeons being shot as part of gun club festivities. He also wanted to know what we, the listeners, considered to be the most obnoxious bird. He was sure there would be plenty of votes from Cape Cod and the islands for the seagull. And he told us how he, the talk show host, tells his children that whenever they see seagulls they should yell: Incoming, Incoming. Because *that*—by which he meant seagull feces—can be a major problem. Next he brought up the crow. The crow, he said, is even nastier and nosier, its call is even more obnoxious than the seagull's. He kept his own council on the matter because he had not yet decided which bird was the most worthless. He wanted to take some calls on the subject and so he asked us, the listeners, if we had ever been irritated by any birds, or if any birds had ever hurt our property values. A construction worker named Patrick called in to say that pigeon feces, when found in buildings that are going to be demolished or rehabbed, are considered hazardous materials. If somebody dumps hazardous material on the highway, the talk show host asked, they could be arrested, right? Patrick screamed, Kill all the pigeons, Kill all the pigeons. The talk show host, who had been interrupted by Patrick, expressed perplexity as to why, on the one hand, it is illegal to dump hazardous materials on the highway, while on the other hand, one could be arrested for shooting pigeons. Look at that pigeon over there, he said. The pigeon was on the fourth floor of City Hall, and the talk show host was certain that it was going to defecate. He then declared that pigeons are not birds, that they are rodents with wings. He recognized that City Hall, which was built in the Stalinist era of architecture, was not the greatest looking building in the world. However, its ambience was certainly not improved by the streaks of pigeon droppings on its walls and windows. And he felt that those people killing pigeons in New York deserved not a prison sentence, but a medal from the city. Instead of worrying about potty parity, he said, the city should give them some kind of medallion for service to society, which they implement by scattering seeds on the sidewalk and capturing with a net those pigeons who come to feed. The pigeons are then driven to Pennsylvania and sold to private gun clubs for live shooting. We then heard the sound of a gun cocking followed by a tremendous explosion. Is Ted in the house, Tattoo, asked the talk show host. This question was followed by a recording of long, deep laughter.

Away

Dear Sir, wasps are circling our heads. Birds watch
our worst moments and their tweets are progress
reports to the wind. Waves are evil yet
they treat some nations more kindly. The news
says the news has disappeared. Still, we are
unsure if fog is our enemy. Wind
is against us. Rumors say fog will join
us. We watch our bodies dissolve into
fog and soon our heads are floating. Our
shadows know where our feet go, our minds do
not. Dear Sir, owls are against us. We
shoot trees but the bullets pierce us. Mud is
against us. Streams are with us. Crickets and
cocoons are against us. Echoes cannot
be tamed. They hide in ditches, or in
perfect visibility. Sleep is not
our friend.

Leek Soup

> *"You can want to do nothing and then decide instead to do this:*
> *make leek soup. Between the will to do something and the will*
> *to do nothing is a thin, unchanging line: suicide."*
>
> —Marguerite Duras

Most people who make leek soup do not make good leek soup
because they do not realize that to make good leek soup
they must realize that instead of making leek soup
they could do nothing. One can only make leek soup by
not wanting to make leek soup. Do not stare into the
leek soup. Stare straight ahead while making leek soup and stir
the soup nonchalantly. A good leek soup smells like
vomit. A bad leek soup tastes like vomit. This is the
challenge of making leek soup: you will want to alter
its nature. But any interest you take in leek
soup will cause it to rebel against you. In this sense,
it is not like pumpkin soup. It is more like a
surly adolescent for whom apathy is a
form of love. Do not insist on making leek soup or
surely you will make bad leek soup. And never say:
tonight I will make leek soup. Do your taxes, or
iron an old shirt. And when leek soup appears, out of
the tedium of your life, do not say: now I will
eat leek soup. People think they know how to eat leek soup.
But they do not know how to eat leek soup because they
do not realize that to eat leek soup they must
realize that instead of eating leek soup they could
do nothing.

The Trouble with Strangers

It was not my dog that bit off the stranger's arm.
I may care for the dog and feed the dog and I
have even paid for her grooming and for her
colorful leash and collar, but does this
entitle me to ownership? I am sorry
for the loss of the stranger's arm and I hope with
all my heart that he will learn to live without it.
But just because I happen to have some
association with the dog—an
association which, despite public accounts,
is far from "intimate"—this does not mean that it
was my boot that broke the stranger's nose. I do not
deny that I am the man on the tape swinging
his leg back and forth. However, what the footage
does not reveal is the aggression the stranger
displayed when I tried to pull his arm out of the
dog's mouth. And even if I did give him one too
many kicks in the face, and even if the lash
on his back came from my whip, it is completely
inaccurate to say that I "brandished it in
a sadistic manner." I was just letting off
some steam, and even if I got a bit carried
away, this does not mean that I used
electrical wires, baseball bats, or candle
wax. I did suggest that the stranger place a
paper bag over his head, but to say that I
forced him to keep it on is a pure abuse
of language. And the cigarette burns on his wrists,
and the socks in his mouth: how could I deny the
requests of a hungry man in pain? True, I tarred
and feathered the stranger, but it wasn't hot tar,
and they weren't real feathers, just synthetic
stuffing.

Postcard from Malibu

after Daniil Kharms and Yedda Morrison

A sexy blow daddy
out of excessive curiosity
looked at a young volcano
a thorn bush
a purple grape
a blue deer
and died
so to speak
a quiet death
in the comfort of his insulating tendency
to fucking want to kill something.
A red-haired man
out of excessive curiosity
found a rat's head
a Barbie doll's leg
identical twins
and died
so to speak
a quiet death
in the comfort of his insulating tendency
to fucking want to kill something.
I walked along the shore,
gnawing away at my own insulating tendencies
until I met a horseman
who
out of excessive curiosity
looked at a blooming hyacinth
a marvelous arm wrestler
a bowl of mashed peas
and died
so to speak
a quiet death
in the comfort of his insulating tendency
to fucking want to kill something.
And the horsemen's horse kicked up some dirt
galloped across the sand
dashed in front of a truck
and died
so to speak
a quiet death
in the comfort of his insulating tendency

to fucking want to kill something.
A veterinarian spoke words of comfort
to a kitty cat with furry whiskers
and went out of his mind.
The veterinarian's assistant
out of excessive curiosity
watched the moon shine white
from the silence of an empty window;
he struck his skull with hammers
and died
so to speak
a quiet death
in the comfort of his insulating tendency
to fucking want to kill something.
A foreigner
out of excessive curiosity
locked himself in a trunk
and died
so to speak
a quiet death
in the comfort of his insulating tendency
to fucking want to kill something.
Darling
my pretty monkey
my plucky plucky
I am sun burnt on the beach.
Kind regards and kisses.

The Hippo-Lexicographer Affair

"It was a mistake."
—Ronald Reagan, Iran-Contra Speech

I did not trade our soybeans for hair pieces, nor
did I trade our confessional poets for Persian
ornithologists. I have issued a directive
prohibiting the undertaking of covert
ornithology. However, I have gasped at
a blue marsh. It was a mistake. And what should
happen when you make a mistake is this: you
diversify your portfolio. You take your
knocks, you learn to ignore the ideologues who
preach that mutual funds are breeding grounds for
Satanists. You know, by the time you reach my age,
you make plenty of mistakes. And if you've lived your
life properly, you diversify your
portfolio. There are reasons why it happened.
And as personally distasteful as I find
secret codes—the pap, as they say, had already
been poured into our ears. I want a pet who is
justifiable and understandable in
public. It was a mistake. And there are reasons
why it happened. For I let my personal
concern for the hippopotamuses spill
over into the geopolitical
strategy of reaching out to the Pan-Asian
lexicographers. I asked so many questions
about the hypothetical human that I
did not ask enough about the specifics of
the total human. Let me say to the
families: I apologize for ignoring
the signals about the thing in question. For I
was so preoccupied with the thing in question
that I forgot about the thing in question. Rest
assured, I have not forgotten about the thing in question.

The Man in Question

They dropped the charges of homicide, filed new charges of
terrorism, dropped the charges of terrorism, filed
new charges of public nudity, dropped the charges of
public nudity, filed new charges of lewd and
lascivious behavior. A spokesman for the FBI
said they found him on the hood of an SUV in a part
of town known as the "Fruit Loop". His penis was in another
man's mouth and in the front seat were vials containing a rare
strand of bacteria known to cause blindness in rats. They
dropped the charges of public nudity and filed new
charges of sodomy. A spokesman for the police department
said they found him with his pants down and it appeared
that his penis was in another man's anus. But since they
could not prove to what degree his penis had penetrated
the other man's anus they dropped the charges of sodomy
and filed new charges of assault and battery. A
spokesman for the Department of Homeland Security said
that he assaulted a worker from the Department of
Public Health who used a Q-tip to extract from inside of
his urethra a rare strand of bacteria capable
of causing pneumonia in chickens. He was placed in
solitary confinement and a spokesman for the
Department of Corrections suggested that he was a
serious threat to the community. They examined the
strand of bacteria found in his urethra but since they
did not properly store the bacteria in the
appropriate container with the appropriate seals and
signatures they could not charge him with intent to commit crimes
against humanity. They dropped the charges of intent to
commit crimes against humanity and filed new charges
of larceny. They said he had stolen the rare strand of
bacteria from his employer and that he had done so
with the deliberate and malicious intent to harm as
many civilians as possible. They tried to verify
for whom he had worked during the given time period but since
they could not verify the name or location of his
employer they dropped the charges of larceny and filed new
charges of tax fraud. When they discovered he was privately
employed, they dropped the charges of tax fraud and filed new
charges of theft with an unregistered weapon. A
grocery store in his neighborhood had recently been robbed
and the cashier said that the thief had carried the same model

of weapon that the man in question kept beneath his bed in
case of emergencies. They dropped the charges of theft with an
unregistered weapon when they discovered the cashier was
partially blind and that the weapon the man in question kept
beneath his bed in case of emergencies had been
properly purchased and registered. When they found on his
bookshelves several works of fiction with blind characters,
including *King Lear*, *Oedipus Rex*, *Endgame*, and *Blindness* by
José Saramago, they accused him of conspiring
to use the rare strand of bacteria to blind not only
the grocer but the seven other blind residents of his
neighborhood, each of whom had had perfectly good eyesight
until he came to town. They asked him why he had so many
books about blindness, but he refused to answer the question.
They asked him why he had so many books about blindness and
when his attorney arrived the man in question said that he
did not know why he had so many books about blindness. They
asked his friends and family why he had so many books
about blindness. No one knew why he had so many books
about blindness and they accused him in the press of
anti-social behavior. When his neighbors testified that
the man in question enjoyed society as much as he
enjoyed a quiet night at home, they dropped the charges of
anti-social behavior. They dropped the charges of
anti-social behavior and filed new charges of
jaywalking. An undercover police officer filmed him
with a video camera as he illegally crossed
the street. At the advice of his attorney, he pleaded
guilty to the charges of jaywalking. He agreed to pay
the fine.

Urban Affairs

We approve of intersections but are opposed to streets in general.

Alleyways and dead ends should be paved over with mountains.

Instead of stop signs, the shadow of a dog, or a hybrid beast with the body of a whale and the head of a turkey.

Out with mayors, in with majordomos.

We prefer aldermen to councilmen, but what we really need are chickens.

Illegal immigrants are taking our jobs. Soon they will take our employers, electrocute their genitals, and eat their children.

We have too many potholes. They should be filled with violets, or ideas.

The Department of Children and Family Services is a front for genetic engineers; they are turning our orphans to lemurs.

Schools are overcrowded. Forty-five pigeons in one classroom: not a proper learning environment.

Landlords have united in their efforts to keep porches from jumping off buildings. Porches are unhappy. They are lining up to collect unemployment. Traffic has never been worse.

Our children have no parks to play in. They play in sewers and eat bleach.

A new initiative on the ballot: replace teachers with fire-hydrants, eliminate the need for air-conditioning.

Illegal immigrants are invading our culture. Soon they will invade our libraries.

Coffins are fleeing the cemetery. They are sick of housing the dead.

Correction

The institution of metaphor making should take
responsibility for punishing makers of metaphor-less
metaphors. And it should be the job of the metaphor maker's
union to propose and carry out laws against the making of
metaphor-less metaphors. These makers of metaphor-less
metaphors are criminals, we say, in the silence of our minds. But
in their baseness these makers of metaphor-less metaphors
justify their actions by saying that we *want* their metaphors, which
are not actually metaphors. Of course, we do want their
metaphor-less metaphors. But just because we want their metaphor
-less metaphors does not mean that we actually want their
metaphor-less metaphors. On the contrary, we want metaphors.
And these makers of metaphor-less metaphors think that because
we want and even enjoy their metaphor-less metaphors that
this must mean that we actually want their metaphor-less
metaphors. The public wants our metaphor-less metaphors, they
say, all the while laughing at how they have fooled us into
thinking that we actually want their metaphor-less
metaphors. Of course, we do not want their metaphor-less
metaphors, but when they speak of cake, which is not actually
cake, they pronounce the words so clearly: Have a slice of cake, say these
corrupt and fraudulent bakers. Have a slice of this moist and fresh,
delicious butter-cream cake. How seduced we are by the clear sound
of their words: Moist and fresh, delicious, butter-cream cake. Moist and fresh,
delicious butter-cream cake. We try to resist the moistness and
freshness of their delicious butter cream cakes, but when they pull out
their shiny knives, and slice into their moist and fresh, delicious
butter cream cakes, we become slaves to the cakelessness of their cakes.
How delicious, we say, as we bite into their moist and fresh,
delicious butter cream cakes. How delicious these butter cream cakes.
We say these words so clearly, and as we savor the moistness and
freshness of their delicious butter cream cakes, we believe in what
we say. But the moment we leave the bakery we cannot help
but chastise ourselves for enjoying their moist and fresh, delicious
butter-cream cakes. These cake-less cakes, we scream, these gastronomic
rejects. These cake-less cakes, we scream, these gastronomic rejects.

Mission Statement

More than anything what I wish to achieve is
for my white shirt to no longer be a symbol
that I must throw myself from the roof. Pleasure is
so unpleasant and yet this same displeasure that
led me once to hide in my
ideological ventures is so pleasing
that I shall invoke the wonders of science to
excavate the beachheads of
cooperation that have led me into this
jungle of suspicion where the dead must be called
the undead. And yet I'm only saying that to
unite myself with myself I must fill
my garden with the flower of civility.
It is a flower of weakness and hard to
digest and though I suffer from fear of words in
general there are words in particular that might
provoke a small change in this life I hate and want.
Oh the gentle sense of peace that comes from the
impossibility of peace. This more than
anything is what I wish to achieve.

For Face

To Suzy

Face, absorbed as you are in cogitation of the glazed
follicle jammed up the earthenware butt of the knickknack
figurine goddess with the head of a bearded Assyrian and the
body of a Golden Retriever with a silky red cravat
hanging from its collar, you do not notice how your nose
twitches to the rhythm of this propitious moment when the
nearly invisible changes in the sky presage this dawn which
will reveal itself to be just another reminder of all
that is vulgar and elegant. And because I am the judge of
the award's ceremony which is our life you shall win the
Nobel Prize for standing and I shall win the Nobel Prize for
sitting, and you shall win the Nobel Prize for anecdotal
hee-haws and I shall win the Pulitzer Prize for making a long
story short, and you shall win the National Book Critics Circle
Award for your masterful interpretations of monkeys and
donkeys and I shall win a Guggenheim Fellowship for my
amphigorically macoronical yum-yums, and you shall
win a MacArthur Genius Grant for your heavenly solitude
that seeks to repair the reputation of the silent
carnival barker who exasperatingly guffaws in my
phlegm as you roast the lemon-basted chicken we will eat
before I ask you to marry me. And in two years time you will
roast another chicken and we will make a baby. And in two
more years you will roast another chicken and we will make
another baby. And soon you will roast another chicken and
we will buy a house in the suburbs even though it violates
my contract as a city employee. And soon you will roast
another chicken and I will carry you on my back and we
will love-love at the mouth of the cave wherein the two dead lovers
of Ur sit naked and tied to a stone bench. And as you reach your
Zanzibarian zenith, dear face, you will whimper in my ear,
"Be bold, my sweet, dream." And as I reach my pinnacle, I will look
into your mouth and say, "Let's get operational, baby." I will dive
into the mossy pits of your humble southern seas.

Why so Pale and Wan, Fond Lover

Baby, the implication of the explication of the
phenomenon of our attraction is that you have forced me to
adopt this punctilious attitude so as to achieve the
impecunious and vicarious application of my
mouth-mouth on your mouth-mouth. Moreover the fact of our mutual
comprehension permits misdeeds to appear as corrective
measures designed to heighten the paradoxical
sublimation of our bilateral miscommunication.
Baby, let us pause for a moment and reflect. For the voices we
hear in the comfort of our carnage grow faint as we enter
the joint-stock company of our accidental
fender-bending fornication. For I have seen your face on the
calm and horrible water and I have lick-licked your
inscrutable tongue-tongue in hopes that the impartial hand of
history will furnish further proof that your lip-lip on my
lip-lip might provide the surprising disillusionment of
poetry. For baby I really love your regressive
deterioration and yes baby I really love the
pyramidal fenestration of your suffocating
resuscitation and yes baby I really heart-heart the
ferocious pettiness of your barbarian bon-bons for they
make me want to crawl like an eel into the algae of your fat
and furry funhouse. For baby I have sucked the
verisimilitude of your kisser and yes baby I have
nip-nipped the reaction-formation of your post-primitive
libidinal reservoir and yes I have nibbled on the
viviparous snake in the succulent labyrinth of your
inner abyss and yes I have fertilized your amorphous
bundle and yes I have even crawled into the
perpendicular nature of your so-called managerial
enhancement package where I have cried ever so softly to the
evanescent shepherds of your fleshless lover and to the strange
birds playing in your saucy, simmering ambivalence.

I tell thee, Dick, where I have been

Pumpkin, if your volcano must open at the foot of
this thy impenetrable puddy then do not look
upon me with that starving gaze of dread. For the prickly
poking of my thin and slippery ding-dong, o pumpkin,
shall cause me soon to plunge the runcible spoon of my
fastidious dinette set into the timorous seed
of Little Martha's smooth and globular thong. O perk-doomed
pumpkin of the ginger-quince felicitous night, do not
engrave your frosty wiggly into this my memory's
hideous chalice. Let me sleep, o pumpkin, let me sleep.
And if your volcano must open, o deep and
cavernous pumpkin, then let the plumage of your
immanent tongue troth so blind upon my firm and fruitful
behind. For I want you not, o pumpkin, to take a bite
out of the charnel-dungeon pang of my pung-pung. O
little pumpkin of the peppy pernicious night, speak to
me of thy hurly-burly fish who soaks in the melting
butter of your wise and virginal crockery. How long
is your finger, o putrefied pumpkin, Do you know how
long is your finger? O chafing pumpkin of the
withering light, embalm this my mind into the still night
of what does not fade when night fades into night. For it is
late my pumpkin. It is too late to talk to the night.

Natural Selection

Darling, the way a wasp larva eats a dead and decaying
caterpillar in a pattern that recalls the ancient English
penalty for treason, I would like to grub your silken cord. And
darling, the way a caterpillar drops suddenly from its leaves
and suspends in the air when attacked by wasps, I would like to
dangle fearfully above your insert until you beep-beep-beep
to signal that I should launch onto your body and muck-muck
the persuasive patina of your pernicious
predetermination. Moreover darling I would like to walk
on the long startled fields of your instinctually
adaptable grass and yes darling I would like to pooh-pooh-poop
on the truculent transmigration of your shadow. For darling
I have teethed on the orchids of your indefinite articles
and yes darling I have pee-peed on the surefooted
evanescence of your experiential hyperbole and
darling let me tell you that when I covet your
famine-encrusted countenance I really covet your
famine-encrusted countenance. For darling I have tickled your
mirth mailbox and darling yes I have love-loved your
hyper-utilitarianism in whose handles I have slurpied
your soft and fluffy vampire butt. For darling the you that you
are is like the I that I was when I was like the you that was
like the me who was hidden in the you of the
impenetrable secrecy of your irretrievable pass
code. For darling I shall chew-chew on your muu-muu and yes darling
I shall sleep in the syntactical marshland of the perfect
forgetfulness of your perfectly forgotten blank.

Maybe I Swerve You

Maybe it's the big neon smock in the grammar of the
lexicographical beast of the insufferable
sagacious Orpheus of the invented noises in the
poverty of your disappearing mythological anti-
language, maybe. Or maybe it's the jealous pool of transplanted
exiles in the angel wings of your nightgown or the
incidental development of narrative in your eyeballs
or the unrecognizable crystalline horizon in the
inaudible echo caused by the friction of your tongue on the
roof of your mouth. Maybe I swerve you for the rapacious
foreshadowing of the incisive propagandistic marshland
in the ascetic lips of your utopian third sex envy.
Or maybe I swerve you for the atavistic wanderer in
your adorable capacity for revenge. Maybe I swerve
the feverishness of the almost touched death jerk in the
momentary trousers of the hermaphroditic egg shells
broken in the purgatorial blades of grass stored in the
erudite anonymity of the trampling neo-logic
of the drowsy foliage of your soft and ominous cheekbones.
Maybe I swerve you for these reasons and for the anointed
abandon of the defenseless pheasant plunging into the
crocodile mouth of the swamp in the silk worm mountains hanging
in the beard on the invisible cum visible deity
in which you and I are but a strand of hair. Yes I most
definitely swerve you for this and for the disjointed
transcendence of the undetectable motion in the
bleeding gladioli warming in the parasitic shadow
of the convalescent sun of your oh so ambiguous bosom.

Diplomacy

You say you love freedom as much as I love freedom you
concupiscent curd but if you really loved freedom as much as
I loved freedom then you wouldn't be such a disco-dancing
disaster you pestilential thug. You say you love freedom you
frog-headed vermin but if you really loved freedom the way I
love freedom then you would be a bigger supporter of
freedom you puny useless tyrant. You say you love freedom you
silly illiterate farm girl but if you really loved freedom
the way you say you loved freedom then you would pull your penis out
of your pants and make love to freedom the way I make love to
freedom you impotent lumpy doorstop. You say you love freedom
you parasitic worm but really you're a freedom-hating
maggot and moreover if you dare step on my dance floor then I
will dropkick your freedom-hating ass in the neck you cyst-covered
four-eyed leper. Take my advice, bozo, if you step once more
on the disco floor my people are going to stick your people's
legacy of courage into the overflowing sewer of
history where your people's pugnacious bards will be eaten by
my people's pugnacious bards you mange-ridden louse-covered cyclops.
And don't tell me you freedom-hating rat that I can't stick my
mother's Santa Claus wherever I want to stick my mother's
Santa Claus because if you really loved freedom you relic from
another era then not only would you really love freedom
but you would really love my mother's Santa Claus you freedom
-hating godless ogre. You think your people know how to dance
better than my people you chuckle-headed bully but if your
people really knew how to dance better than my people you
genital wart then your people wouldn't be starving and
moreover you wouldn't look like such a dinosaur when you do
the mambo you lonely stagnant oppressor. You say you love
freedom you epileptic squid but you don't love freedom because
if you did love freedom then maybe my people would let your
people buy our people's crops you malnourished freedom-hating
pervert. I love freedom. Do you want to know why I love freedom?
I love freedom because I really love freedom. But you don't love
freedom. Because if you really loved freedom the way I really
loved freedom you turd-lipped goat-fucking llama then you would show a
little bit more love for freedom you free-balling voodoo-dicked coward.
And that's the truth, old buddy. That's the god-damned real *verdad*.

Desire: 7 Modules

"Never drive a car when you're dead."
— Tom Waits

Pharmaceutical Module

I can't make it with you, baby,
because the demands of the chemical insurgency
have decelerated your ability
to make a mountain out of my molehill.
I want to make it with you, baby,
but my brigade is not deployable.

Historical Module

I want to make it with you, baby,
but my squadron does not have the aptitude
to penetrate your fortress.
I want to make it with you,
but the great sweep of human history
is no longer on my side.

Inflationary Module

I want to make it with you, baby,
but misguided central planning
has led to a pervasive misallocation of capital.
The central bank is closed, baby,
and I can not make a deposit.

Incentives-based Module

I want to make it with you, baby,
but I can not actualize the potential
of my unilateral morphology mechanism.
I need subsidies, baby,
to achieve my intended goal.

Biological Module

I want to make it with you, baby,
but I can not allow you
to inspect my factory.
My mobile lab has been looted, baby;
my missile only shoots blanks.

Privatization Module

I really want to make it with you, baby,
but my resources are not sufficient.
You must implement an innovative policy
to stimulate my private sector.

Cosmetic Module

I want to make it with you, baby,
but you look so good
and I feel so great
that any further action
would permanently dismantle
my weapons-launching capacity.

To His Coy Mistress

Baby, I know that when you're not with me, you don't
think about me, but baby, when you are with me,
it's like, whoa, I mean, before I knew you, I had
always wanted passion with an emotional
connection, but baby, until I met you, I
had no idea that deeper feelings were
actually important. Baby, until I
met you, I had either great sex with random chicks
or so-so sex with serious girlfriends. But baby,
you are totally different. Not only
am I proud to bring you home to my parents, but
baby I really love it when we play dress up,
and try different positions, and have sex in
public places. When you're naughty, baby, it
doesn't make me think less of you; it only makes
me love you more.

Dick Cheney's Mistress

I watched a really cute zookeeper give his tiger a scratchy
scratchy and I got jealous because I wanted a scratchy
scratchy but I couldn't tell him I wanted a scratchy
scratchy because even though this morning I blow-dried upside
down and finished with a light hold constructor spray, because
even though I spent hours trying to maximize every strand
with a light mist and a spray-on gel, today I have hair from hell.

Dick likes it when I do that thing his ex-girlfriend used to do.
Generally speaking, I have a rule about this, but rules
are meant to be broken, so I tell Dick that size doesn't
matter, which really gets him hot.

Two weeks ago, I suggested Dick use a male
enlargement system, and for a few short days I was amazed as
his penis grew into the biggest, thickest, hardest one I'd
ever had. I told Dick I would remember his penis
forever. Then he stopped taking the pills and shrunk back to his
small old self. At first I pretended not to miss the
vigorous thrust I had received from his juiced-up Johnson, though
of course I did miss the sheer intensity and
concentrated power of the orgasms I had had the
week before. But how do you tell a guy you're not that
into him because his package is too small? As Lyndon
Johnson used to say, Just wait for the right moment and pounce. Like
for example, last night when he mentioned Benazir Bhutto,
the former Prime Minister of Pakistan. It's one thing to
feel like you don't measure up to some dippy model, I screamed
hysterically, but a sexy Prime Minister is
really threatening. Another time, during cunnilingus,
Dick asked about the scar on my belly, to which I
responded by telling him I had a C-section when I
gave birth to the baby I gave up for adoption when I
was sixteen. In other words, Dick, let your boner rest in peace.

Only the Names have been Changed to Protect the Innocent

Into wanted to go onto Onto's into
But Onto did not want Into in his into
He wanted Into on his onto
So he said to Into
Why don't you go onto my onto

Because your onto is not as warm as your into, said Into
And though your into is not as warm as my into
An into needs more than his own into, said Into
An into needs the warmth of another's into

And an onto needs the warmth of another's onto, said Onto
And though often I go onto my own onto, said Onto
It is warmer on your Onto

I will not let you onto my onto, said Into
But I am happy to let you into my into

Blood of unrequited love
To whom do you flow
Sang the chorus

As Onto tried to get onto Into's onto
And Into tried to get into Onto's into

But neither Into nor Onto
Could get into or onto
The object of their desire

Blood of unrequited love
To whom do you flow
Sang the chorus

Who proposed a compromise
By suggesting to Onto
That perhaps Into would let him onto his onto
If he agreed to let Into into his into

And Into, sang the chorus
Perhaps Onto will let you into his into
If you let Onto onto your onto

I will let Into into my into, said Onto
But how do I know that Into
Will let me onto his onto

Which is to say, said Into
That if I let Onto onto my onto
Before he lets me into his into
How do I know he won't flee

And since it was impossible for Into
To go into Onto's into
At the same time as Onto
Went Onto Into's onto
Onto and Into
Were asked by the chorus
To put something up for collateral
To guarantee their mutual gratification

But what? said Onto

My n, said Into

And my n, said Onto

Who was now called Oto
And Into was now called Ito

A coin was flipped
And when Oto won
He went onto Ito's onto
Then Ito went into Oto's into

Blood of unrequited love
To whom do you flow
Sang the chorus

For now that Oto and Ito
Had attained their desire
Neither found satisfaction
For both felt
That the attainment of desire
Was not as pleasurable
As the longing for unattainable desire

Poem for my Mutual Fund

again for Mark Booth

Oh mutual fund, I used to be scared of the free market; I
used to think the free market was like a beast with a lion's
body and the head of a man, and the mouth of a frog and the
skin of a snake, and the lips of a hippopotamus and the
nose of a lexicographer, and whose fingers were fiddler crabs,
and whose ears were plugged with wax so they would not hear the cauldron of
boiling armadillos in its belly. And its veins were
aphids, and its nipples were wolverines, and its heart was the paw
of a chimpanzee, and its penis was a caterpillar, and
its knuckles were basenjis. And its left butt cheek was a
bioflavonoid, and its right butt cheek a mountain goat. And its
mouth was Vanessa Redgrave, and its arms were plankton and its teeth
a red bone. But now, dear mutual fund, I no longer think so
bleakly of the market. For with the help of drugs that target my
amygdala, which is a brain structure essential for
decoding emotions, particularly threatening
stimuli, I am no longer nervous about investing. Oh
mutual fund, you have beta-blockers to thank for the
elimination of market-fear in my amygdala; you
have Xanax and Nardil to thank for the
$1,777 that as
of today, February 12, 2006, have accrued in your tax-free
shelter. Oh mutual fund, your bravery in the face of a
turbulent market reminds me of the year
1777, when, on August 27th,
William Alexander, also known as Lord Stirling, who had been
a miserable failure at the art of making money, but
whose military genius was never in doubt, led a
battalion of Marylanders into defeat at the hands of
Cornwallis. Over 400 soldiers died, oh mutual fund,
but Lord Stirling's decision to attack at Long Island preserved
the integrity of Washington's command and allowed our troops
to win the war. Oh mutual fund, you remind me of
Washington and his brave soldiers who on Christmas Day
1777 ate soggy fire-cake and
carrion as they wintered at Valley Forge in the nadir of
the revolution. Oh Fidelity Low-Priced Mutual Fund, stick things in me
as I stick things in you; track my growth as I track the growth in you.

The Barbaric Writers

"This is my last communiqué from the planet of the monsters."
Roberto Bolaño, *Distant Star*

When I watched the Barbaric Writers defecate on my
manuscript, I felt a great sense of relief, a great sense of
fraternity with these men who loved literature enough to
destroy it, and I recalled a poem I had once written, but
never had the confidence to publish, about a so-called
poet who shat himself into a toilet, only to float on his
back as torrential downpours of poetry filled the bowl and drowned
him. I have always known that constipation is essential to
poetry, though what I did not realize, until recently,
was that poetry itself is repulsive. Words on their own are
bad enough. But when placed alongside other words, when formed
into rhythmic lines and stanzas: no act of creation is more
hideous. In the salons, I have often watched, before my turn
came on, our local poets reciting their verses. They speak
politely, and with grace, to an audience that sips wine and
chuckles at the words that flow not from their mouths, but from their
plugged-up behinds. What a holy mockery of literature!
Were the barbarians to see such a spectacle, no
theater walls could stand the shock of their laughter. No, poetry
is not what I want. Only defecation on poetry. For
after years of humiliation, I have finally learned that
to humanize our poems, we must shit on them. We must shit
freely, with arms raised, as detectives in blue sport coats examine
our feces for sustainability, all the while fighting
off other detectives in bluer sport coats who take our
poetic leakage to their laboratories to search for
parasitic demons, or diamonds, depending on the angle.
We smear what drips from our self-inflicted wounds onto our verses,
combining blood and ink into new poetic forms in which we
rub our faces, the better to smell our disgusting children with,
the better to drool on our disgusting children with; and once we
have bled and drooled and driveled, we declare our poems complete, the
better to wipe our asses with, before submitting them for
publication. We smear our typewriters with pus and semen, and
chastise any fool crass enough to declare himself a poet,
an offense punishable by confinement in a cage
surrounded by Barbaric Writers who expectorate between
the distinguished author's eyes, his hands tied behind his back to
prevent him from cleaning his face. For poetry is hard work! It
is hard to create such filthy, vile putrescence.

The Forest of Barbaric Sestinas

for Roberto Bolaño

The barbaric writer tried to write a barbaric sestina
about his inability to write a barbaric sestina, but in the end
he could not write a sestina about his inability to write
a sestina, he could only write a sestina about his desire
to defecate on all the sestinas he had ever read, which were almost always about love
and its opposite—poetry—which he first encountered in the forest

as a child when he witnessed a wolf eating a kitten. In the forest,
the cracking lilacs turned to mold, and the sestina
about his inability to write a barbaric sestina became a sestina about his love
for defecating on poems about trees, mountains, rivers, and the ends
of seasons; he liked urinating on Robert Frost, but when it came to Rilke, his desire
was to vomit all over the *Sonnets to Orpheus*, especially the one where Rilke writes

of the cycles of flowers and fruit, which always made the barbaric writer
think of an empty space, an empty forest that contains all other forests
wherein the barbaric writer disguises himself as a barbaric writer who desires
the complete obliteration of language, a difficult subject for a sestina,
though who has not dreamed of writing a silent poem with no end,
for when we write about murder, thought the barbaric writer, we are actually writing
                                                                about love.

The barbaric writer hated poems in general, but he could not suppress his love
for poems about his hatred for poetry. So he began to write
about his desire to destroy poetry, but in the end
he wrote such beautiful poetry about his hatred for poetry that he could not see the forest
for the trees, for the leaves were filled with villanelles, sonnets, and sestinas
about his barbaric alter-ego who desired nothing more than to not desire what he most
                                                                desired,

and what he most desired, or so he thought, was to defecate on Baudelaire and Keats, a
                                                                desire
to be realized by abandoning the ideals of truth and beauty, and asserting instead that love
is like vomiting on Goethe and Henry James in the same sestina.
Thus the barbaric writer began his sestina with the words, Today I write
because I cannot vomit or defecate, I can only walk through the forest
and urinate on Shakespeare, Flaubert, Cervantes, Whitman, and even Dante, for the end

of poetry will be achieved only when ordinary barbarians, like you and I, unite to end
the practice of admiring texts, and replace it with the desire
to destroy texts in ceremonies of blood, vomit, defecation, and book burnings in forests.
But there remained the problem of love,
for though he wanted to have no affectionate feelings for poetry, the barbaric writer
could see only beauty in the hatred that filled every word of his sestina

about the end of poetry.   The barbaric writer loved hatred, and hated love,
nevertheless, he knew that his desire for love, and not hatred, had inspired him to write
the Forest of Barbaric Sestinas in the forest of barbaric sestinas.

They Turned their Attention to Bras

They either have paddings that push my boobs up so high I'm suffocating, said the National Security Adviser, or they strap them down, resulting in a flattened pancake effect. The Secretary of State twirled like a ballerina, looked into the mirror, and said, I'm shapely and I don't like wearing skimpy stuff, but this robe is the best—it's silky and clingy and the belt accents my waist. People are so wise, said the Secretary of Defense, that they prop a ladder against the sun, and pretend to be apple sauce. Dressed in punky casual pants with pointy red pumps, his retro look was causing quite a stir in the Beltway. By law, said the Attorney General, the bra must lift and separate perfectly. A legal adviser suggested that breasts and bras be reviewed on a case-by-case basis. But the Attorney General was steadfast in his belief that the rights of breasts should be treated only in general terms. The pancake bras must be detained, he screamed. He smoothed the fabric of his animal print camisole, and when the Chief of Staff entered wearing a colorful kimono, he threw his hands up in disgust. America is being inundated with cherry blossoms and geishas, the Attorney General said. It's because of their soothing, Zen-like effect, said the President. But the question remains, said the Attorney General— and it is indeed a troubling one—Is this the kind of formal wear we ought to promote? Comfort, shouted the National Security Adviser, should be our administration's top priority. The Attorney General bristled.

Sentence

Ain't nothing more beautiful than a French diplomat in an
Italian suit discussing the intimate ties between
poetry and constipation with a United States
Senator in a discount blazer from the Men's Wearhouse bought
especially for the occasion of proposing the
Anti-Chimera Act, a prime indicator that if children were
once the future, they are now the past, which is growing
hairier every moment, so as to keep us from
penetrating its insides, which we must nibble on as if
nibbling on donuts, by which I mean rubrics, glittering
rubrics in the dry heat of an empty test bank full of
raccoons with flexible snouts and long tails that
materialize in the shrubbery as thick-set stocky
fraternity brothers suicide bomb colleges full of free
thinking mavericks with tuning forks in their ears and rubber dicks
in their pockets, a veritable cure for loneliness and
its side effects, including the desire to fantasize
about mythological genitalia in the pants of
pundits who declare that to be alive is
fundamentally okay as long as poets test their
verses on guinea pigs before submitting them to us
humans as we exit the amalgamated marshland of
surplus value and enter an ordinary evening on
which ordinary people dream of lubricated condoms
for dogs, of mules who practice the pull-out method, of birth
control pills for cats, of floating trousers that haunt city squares
in search of red-walled boutiques where silk stockings and boot-cut
chinos fight for the attention of disembodied legs
while merchants masturbate, aroused by visions of painless
castration, aroused by hands without arms scribbling conjunctions
into dusty ceilings, aroused by hands without arms stirring
infinite bowls of soup, aroused by module-makers who
insist only on the metaphorical value of money
as represented in the hieroglyphics painted on the
walls of financiers who accumulate capital through the
unjustified sexual behavior of adulterous
women who appear asymmetrically—legs over heads, hands
coming out of butts—in public ceremonies in which
syringes suck out erroneous feelings from their bodies
while suits and ties stuff bones and ears into decorative
bottles and jars.

Market Ideology

after Shakespeare

When I do not count the clock that tells the time
and think of rodents in the mashed potatoes at Roosevelt High,
when Molotov cocktails explode in violins
and Choriomeningitis grows in hamster droppings,
when acid drips on perinea and coccyges
and cyanide is discovered in cartons of juice
and when the perfect sleeves of technocrats
sway forces beyond the control of the market,
I will dream this night
of the sorrows of your changing face
as you monitor the oscillations
of the turbulent Tokyo Stock Exchange.

When I do not count the clock that tells the time,
and stare instead at the perfect imperfection of the sea
which washes transparent horses to the shore
whose glittering intestines remind me
of my inability to outwit the numinous logic of late capitalism,
I will not misread this vision
as a sign that my dividends will bust
but I will dream this night of shepherds and artichokes
and think of my portfolio
(a firm and salty bottom)
as I ejaculate on my financial forecast
for the following fiscal year.

The Shrinking Island

The invisible weight of the future is strapped to the wings of the bird trapped inside the gutter of the flat roof on which the family of fourteen sleeps. The men who eat their own skin have prayed in such a way that the young girls of the island will have varicose veins by their tenth birthday. The rumbling of chemicals in my stomach is another sign that I belong to the tribe that does not belong. I could tell by looking at her face that she wasn't fertile. I knew right away that her older brother had thrown her baby into the river. That everything I say or think is a question of voice is undermined by the movements of my body. I sink into myself more and more each time I open my mouth, she said, and I sink out of myself each time I close my mouth. Each time I speak, she said, I become a little bit more and a little bit less like myself. The filthiest word to the residents of the island is visible. They do not care for what they can see. They do not want to see what they can see. For four days I ran around the island looking for a view of nothing. I finally found one atop the noodle shop in the easternmost part of the easternmost province. The four-fingered man who owns the noodle shop brought tea and special glasses that turn the air the color of smoke. I was ecstatic. I wanted nothing more than to see nothing other than an island of dust and smoke.

The amount of fish in the water is dwindling. Those who survived the floods and chemical spills no longer have spines. To see a spineless fish floating in the ocean is to see all that is human about nature. At the kiosk outside the pharmacy that caters to foreigners, twenty-seven types of consolation are available for the low cost of misery or the high cost of happiness. Yesterday we walked for three hours and still did not find the type of cobblestone we were looking for. We did not want to go inside any churches or museums. We wanted to be outside with the people, searching for the sacred cobblestone. We searched the entire island for the beige pebbles that are said to bring good health when placed inside the mouth of the sick. Legend says a legless boy grew his legs back after swallowing a handful of beige pebbles and washing them down with tea made from lemon and rosehips. On a billboard, a primitive man with a bubble coming out of his mouth asks if Jesus died on a stake, a cross, or a tree. The museum in the underground torture chambers holds the answer to this question. We considered visiting the underground torture chambers but were afraid we would never want to ascend. Two tight-rope walkers walk the tight-rope that crosses the entire span of the island. One walker starts on one side, the other starts on the other side. When they meet in the middle, they make love, orgasm, and die, so to speak, a quiet death, in the service of their god, their families, and their nation. To die in service of your nation is more honorable than to die in service of yourself. We spent the entire evening watching a woman blow butterflies out of her mouth while juggling a kitten, a cantaloupe, and a water snake. We spent the entire day inside the cave that houses the pubic hair of the martyred soldiers. However, the parade of virgins was a total snore. The little boys hid inside the white dresses of the virgins and pretended to be birthed immaculately. Tennis, anyone?

When the enormous bucket brought us down to the bottom of the sacred well, she held my hand between her hands and told me that this was just like her childhood. Everything I like about myself is contained in the words I love you, she said, as she crawled into the sewer to search for the diaphragm she had hid the night before. On the shrinking island, they do not care for prophylactics. In 1983, a man had his penis removed for wrapping it in a condom. The condom-covered penis, preserved now in formaldehyde, is encased in glass in the private chambers of the judiciary, where it is seen only by movie stars and diplomats, who are said to take great pleasure in photographing it for their friends and families. For fourteen dollars and eighty-three cents, you can watch iguanas copulate at the zoo. For twenty-three dollars and thirty-eight cents, you can watch iguanas, squirrels, beavers, axolotls, and various sea creatures copulate in the private copulation chambers of the zoo. We paid full-price to watch the animals copulate at the zoo, and we did not regret our decision. Afterwards, we went back to our hotel room, stripped off our clothes, made love, orgasmed, and died, so to speak, a quiet death, in the comfort of our insulating tendencies to fucking want to kill something. Behind the castle, throngs line up to watch cats chase rabbits. The interconnectedness of everything and nothing rings truer each time you tell me I have an awful sense of direction. Everything I like about myself has already happened, she said, as she watched the shaman set himself on fire. As night fell, we sat in the rain eating pastries in the sacred garden of silence. When the sun appeared, the flowers flew away.

The Heart is a Lonely Perineum

For Anna and Jimmy

And if it is true that all I can do is float
through these tunnels of dust and pain in which
capital swims in the arms of mercilessness,
then I will put you in the coffin I wear
around my waist and bind you with a rose to the
small triangular bone at the end of my
spinal column where the you that is not you shall
meet the you that might be you and together we
will form a family who will flourish inside this
golden abyss whose entryway is guarded by
a gaggle of slithering creditors with
pee-pees for guns and Chinese porcelain for
eyeballs. For who is to say that the air we breathe
is anything more than a secret code both
capricious in structure and marketable in
the substance of its sad and tender humility.
I was teaching the Laotians about the
existential implications of the
conditional voice when a man came on the
loudspeaker and said we were all a bunch of
Mexican widows with secret Jewish husbands
in our titties. A woman in a velvet dress
jumped out of the rosemary bush and showed us
how to hide those we have murdered in our bodies. I
did not know the blind were invisible to
themselves until I chopped up an old harpy, shoved
her into my underpants, and chuckled as she
struggled to put herself back together. Then we
hopped into my Hybrid Honda Civic and sped
across the border to the all-you-can-eat
rotisserie chicken shack whose drive-thru window
clerk is the Virgin Mary on whose lips you must
tap three times before telling her there is a
handful of dust on her posterior vulva
junction, at which point she will become all the
women you should have kissed but didn't. This will come
true, even if you don't believe it.

Exile

And soon the city will be an abandoned house, then a
ditch, then a forest. And the forest will be filled with clowns
you will sense but not see. And these clowns, who are you, will
remove your skin inch by inch until you are nothing but
bone. The forest will be empty, and you will be cold,
transparent, and alone, which will allow you to keep
living because you will have the presence to explain your
absence, and to know that love is like a cistern full of
little boys laughing at a city of Byzantine
knickknacks on the icy bank of an empty shore where the
lucid salesmen have no words and where the smog shields
the crumbling cliffs on the edge of town near the drive-in
movie theatre that perpetually plays the
drama about the clown who can not go to the ball
unless he wears his big red boots and wig, and gets fat with
the grandeur of knowing himself for what he is not: a
splendid jumble of wit, charm, and guile.

A Wounded Deer Leaps Highest

after Emily Dickinson

I have apprehended the sound of a person pursuing animals give the account of a ruminant mammal, whose body has been injured by violence, whose skin has been lacerated, its membranes broken, spring free from the ground, passing abruptly from one state to another, showing the greatest degree of upward extension, advancing towards the culmination, rising up into an excited or stupefied state, into a region of high barometric pressure.

This is merely a mystic or prophetic trance, a rapturous delight caused by the permanent cessation of all vital function, lasting only until the motion arrester, its friction quelled, is devoid of gesture.

The mineral matter that has been struck sharply emits a sudden, copious flow; the crushed iron that leaps or jumps suddenly: the fleshy side of the face invariably resembling the hue of blood when the fever pierces with poison.

Laughter is the postal system of those who suffer intense sorrow, in which their admonished upper limbs, fearing that one might secretly catch sight of the fluid that circulates in the heart, will cry out, that the one being addressed feels pain.

Sonnet for a moor

after Pablo Neruda

A sparrow, a moor, violet coronas, and dada;
Mother, I'll entertain your passionate hairy sadists,
lunch on your last dollars, coordinate your lace collars,
put cake on your nose and ego, and steam up your almonds.

Parquet precipice, taste of tofu, eggs, velour, roses;
deep ruts in the trellis, the oaks freeze, as does my canine.
The floor, the petals, the human monster of my mirage:
can we unseat those pasts caught hopelessly in our levees?

Your ghost is lost. Your house trembles and aches, paves, orates to
the yellow ball; it dazzles and poses, murmurs and yells:
to establish an angel, suppress the celestial.

My entrails quell the cruel moor; my circus bakes in its guts;
hats off, quick, and lacerate my dome: cones and spades to bridge
my broken reason: for uncle is   my naughty auntie.

Hannah and Gary in the Garden State

The Jewish woodcutter who doubled as a professional wrestler lived in a caged wrestling rink that from a certain angle looked like the Tropicana Casino in Atlantic City only it had more windows and not enough room for his third wife and his two children Hannah and Gary who looked more like experimental poets than most experimental poets only they were not on the tenure track and they preferred Frank O'Hara to Louis Zukofsky and could not give a shit about Robert Duncan or Charles Olson but preferred Georges Perec and Busta Rhymes. The woodcutter's third wife was a native of New Jersey who called her bra a hat for the twins and who did not know her way around the wrestling rink which she called a roller skating rink and she did not like wrestling but preferred roller derby and was not very nice to Hannah and Gary who she called Leroy and Marguerite as she confused them with her two cats Lee and Maggie who looked like militant members of the French Resistance and who left home at the age of three to join the East Coast Gypsies who kidnapped small children by reeling them in with lovable cats who when touched by kind children unleashed a spell that made the children want to be kidnapped and used as ransom for cash rewards far beyond the means of their parents who had to sell all their possessions in order to buy back their children who because they were from New Jersey looked like Allen Ginsberg only without the beard and bongos.

The Jewish woodcutter's third wife who was in the Witness Protection Program and whose name was Cardamom Kinashawa declared one day that there was not enough rubber on the floor of the wrestling rink and there were not enough wrestling leotards for the whole family and so she tried to convince her husband who had the head of Henry Kissinger the body of Jennifer Aniston and the feet of Andre the Giant to put Hannah and Gary up for adoption and she knew just the perfect gay couple who really wanted kids and who lived in Hoboken because they had been priced out of Manhattan Brooklyn Queens the Bronx and even Staten Island after they lost their jobs as hit men for the mob when it was revealed that they were having sex with corpses before dumping them in the

East River but the Jewish woodcutter who believed in traditional family values did not think that Carlo the Finger and Sammy the Mouth-Mouth would be the best caretakers for Hannah and Gary whom he loved and loved and loved.

There are not enough leotards for Hannah and Gary said Cardamom Kinashawa one day to her husband who was not paying attention to his wife because he was reading Jean Lyotard in a leotard and theorizing as to what effect the rubber bands in Captain Lou Albano's beard may have had on his election into the Professional Wrestling Hall of Fame.

There is not enough rubber on the floor of the wrestling rink screamed Cardamom Kinashawa who grew up a protestant in Newton Massachusetts and who as a child summered on Martha's Vineyard and in the south of France before losing her own parents in a double-suicide (white-collar embezzlers) at which point she was moved from foster family to foster family never finding one for whom she was a perfect fit thus at the age of 16 she ran away and started a life of crime first counterfeiting US currency then as a call girl before embarking upon a tragically short career as a cocktail waitress for a mafia-run nightclub which ended with her arrest and testimony that led to indictments against some of the east coast's most notorious bosses.

Said Cardamom Kinashawa: If you do not agree to let Carlo the Finger and Sammy the Mouth-Mouth adopt Hannah and Gary then we must put them in the new incinerator in Monmouth County which was opposed by radical members of the medical community who feared the toxicological effects the incinerator would have on ordinary citizens like you and me.

Everyone knew there was an impoverished Mexican Mariachi band who lived at the bottom of the Monmouth County incinerator and so the professional wrestling Jewish woodcutter thought for a moment that perhaps it was not such a bad idea to throw his children into the incinerator as they might be able to find a good trade and a good home with these renowned musicians who could be seen on summer nights playing the boardwalk in Asbury Park.

One evening Hannah overheard Cardamom Kinashawa trying to convince her father to put them in the incinerator; she comforted her brother Gary:

Don't worry said Hannah who kept a red wheelbarrow in her blouse because she knew that so much depended on her being able to carry her brother from one end of the state to the other in case their parents abandoned them. If they stick us in the incinerator we will find our way back home.

She filled her pockets with argumentative essays then slipped into bed where she dreamed of orchids and plums and loose suburban housewives who were stocked day and night by sexy encyclopedia salesmen who looked like Dustin Hoffman and Al Pacino in the early days of their careers.

The next day Cardamom Kinashawa put a chemical sedative into the Jewish woodcutter's rice pudding and he slept for two and a half days. Cardamom Kinashawa then stole a sports utility vehicle from the parking lot of a local gas station. She threw Hannah and Gary into the rear and drove to the Monmouth County incinerator and as they traveled the depths of the Garden State Parkway Hannah dropped her argumentative essays out of the window and said a prayer to still the wind so that her essays would not blow away.

Dear Air said Hannah who looked like Meg Ryan prior to plastic surgery. Today you will not have wind. Instead you will be filled with the scent of beef tacos my favorite food.

And so the wind was stilled and the air was filled with the scent of tacos and throughout the Garden State Parkway there were argumentative essays that Hannah had composed for the early college class she was taking nights when she finished her shift at Baskin Robbins where she went each day after high school in order to help her father afford the rent for his wrestling rink. And when they finally arrived at the Monmouth County incinerator Cardamom Kinashawa punched out Hannah and Gary and hired two hobos to throw them in the dump for which she repaid them by sucking on their ears and penises.

Now you will burn chortled Cardamom Kinashawa who wore shiny red pumps and a leopard spotted wrestling leotard. Now you will burn you rat-faced Jewish snots with Tic Tacs for brains and gummy bears for DNA.

But Cardamom Kinashawa did not know the special feature of the Monmouth County incinerator: it was programmed to reject the scent of human flesh: a measure negotiated by an immigrant rights group advocating on behalf of the Mexican Mariachis.

Cardamom Kinashawa drove away in the sports utility vehicle. Meanwhile inside the incinerator Hannah and Gary awoke and met Epiphanio and Dionisia the son and daughter of New Jersey's most impoverished Mariachi couple Dionisio and Ephiphania who looked like Demi Moore and Rob Lowe in the film *About Last Night* only they were shorter and darker. Epiphanio and Dionisia immediately befriended Hannah and Gary and taught them how to play Mariachi music. Hannah played the trombone and Gary played the guitar and when the incinerator ignited the four children were ejected through the escape hatch and onto the pavement. Hannah pulled the wheelbarrow out of her blouse. Gary jumped in and with Epiphanio and Dionisia at their sides they began their journey across New Jersey following the trail of argumentative essays that Hannah had scattered across the Garden State Parkway.

Abortion: Do you agree or disagree with the legality of abortion? Defend your argument with relevant supporting details.

The Death Penalty: Do you agree or disagree with the death penalty? Defend your argument with relevant supporting details.

School Uniforms: Do you think public school students should wear uniforms? Defend your argument with relevant supporting details.

Hannah picked up her first essay and quickly slipped it into her skirt pocket for she did not want Epiphanio and Dionisia to see her argument as she was pro-choice and since she assumed that Epiphanio and Dionisia were devout Catholics she feared they might oppose her and this was certainly not the time to alienate their new friends with quarrels about

God and politics. But Epiphanio and Dionisia could not read which Hannah and Gary discovered when they stopped for lunch at a diner in Little Silver. Epiphanio was upset because he wanted a fish sandwich but the picture he pointed to on the menu was of a chicken sandwich and he did not eat chicken because it made him want to puke his guts out.

We must teach you to read said Hannah when she discovered that Epiphanio and Dionisia were illiterate. When we get back to our wrestling rink said Hannah we will teach you to read. We will begin with the classics: Goethe, Plato, and Aristophanes then we can move on to the *USA Today, The National Enquirer* and the novels of John Le Carré and Haruki Murukami.

This was a kind offer but it has little relevance to the story except perhaps that it made the music that flowed from Epiphanio and Dionisia's instruments all the more joyous as they traveled the Garden State Parkway where argumentative essays gleamed in the moonlight (*Prayer in School; Universal Health Care; Mandatory Sterility for Sex Offenders*) leading the children back home. They crept in through a small hole without waking Cardamom Kinashawa. Cold and tired but thankful to be home again Hannah and Gary put on their leotards (they did not have enough for Epiphanio and Dionisia) and slipped into bed.

The next day when Cardamom Kinashawa discovered that Hannah and Gary had returned with Epiphanio and Dionisia she was so upset that she took out a switch blade carved up her thighs and wrote an entry into her web log about how after inventing Hannah and Gary she no longer wanted them to exist but she had forgotten the code for de-inventing them and now she was stuck with these two butt crack kids and their raggletaggle Mexican friends who smelled like sewage and cheese toast.

Meanwhile in the parlor of the wrestling rink which looked like a western style saloon Epiphanio and Dionisia were teaching Hannah and Gary how to play *El Rey* but Cardamom Kinashawa was so offended by the music that she took a hammer struck

Epiphanio and Dionisia repeatedly on their skulls and locked their dead bodies in the army chest she kept in the cellar beneath the wrestling rink at which point the Jewish woodcutter awoke from his slumber and said to his family that our state and yours will be really awake and not merely dreaming like most societies with their shadow battles and struggles for political power which they treat as some great big prize. He then went on the internet and downloaded pornography to which he masturbated before striking his wife with the same hammer she had used to kill Epiphanio and Dionisia.

He sang: It's a hard knock's life for us. It's a hard knock's life for us.

But what he meant was that he never should have married Cardamom Kinashawa in the first place and so to make up for his wrongs he built Hannah and Gary a house made of nougat and vanilla wafer and stuck inside of it an old witch who was friendly but preferred eating children to seeing the children eat candy thus she tried to force the children to clean the cobwebs out of her behind but the children said where is your behind and so when she bent down to show them her behind they kicked her in the stomach gagged her and threw her in the back of the sports utility vehicle Cardamom Kinashawa had stolen the previous day. Hannah and Gary stuck Cardamom Kinashawa's switch blade to their father's throat and demanded he drive to the Monmouth County incinerator but instead of throwing the old witch in the incinerator they ripped out her nose and eye balls and shoved them into her mouth and then they cut off her ears and fingers and shoved them into her arm pits. The woodcutting Jewish father ejaculated with such force that he broke his back which did not make Hannah and Gary sad. On the contrary the events of the previous days had convinced Hannah and Gary that their father was as worthless as Cardamom Kinashawa and so they pulled out every hair on his head and they ripped out his finger nails and shoved frogs into his mouth until he could no longer breathe then they dumped his body into the incinerator. Hannah and Gary knew that such an act had the power to bring the dead back to life but Epiphanio and Dionisia did not come back to life. Epiphanio and Dionisia could have come back to life thanks to the frogs that Hannah and Gary had shoved into their father's mouth but they chose to not come back to life because they never liked life that much living as they were in the

Monmouth County incinerator and so they decided to swim forever in the murky river of the dead. They took the road less traveled and that made all the difference.

Made in the USA